VICTORY IN EUROPE

by

Wallace B. Black
and
Jean F. Blashfield

CRESTWOOD HOUSE
New York

Maxwell Macmillan Canada
Toronto

Maxwell Macmillan International
New York Oxford Singapore Sydney

Library of Congress Cataloging-in-Publication Data

Black, Wallace B.
  Victory in Europe / by Wallace B. Black and Jean F. Blashfield. —
1st ed.
      p.   cm. — (World War II 50th anniversary series)
  Includes index.
    Summary: Recounts how the Allied forces defeated Germany in World War II.
    ISBN 0-89686-570-3
    1. World War, 1939-1945 – Campaigns – Europe – Juvenile literature [1.
World War, 1939-1945 – Campaigns – Europe.] I. Blashfield, Jean F.
II. Title. III. Series: Black, Wallace B.
World War II 50th anniversary.
D743.B493   1993
940.54'21—dc20

                                                                    92-23234

Created and produced by B & B Publishing, Inc.

Picture Credits
Dave Conant (map) - page 19
National Archives - pages 3, 4, 7, 10, 12, 14, 21, 22, 24, 25, 26, 27, 28, 29, 31, 32, 34, 35, 37, 39, 41,
    43, 45 (both)
Soufoto - pages 15, 16, 17, 18
United States Air Force - page 11

CRESTWOOD   Macmillan Publishing Company   Maxwell Macmillan Canada, Inc.
HOUSE   866 Third Avenue   1200 Eglinton Avenue East
                     New York, NY 10022   Suite 200
                                                        Don Mills, Ontario M3C 3N1

Macmillan Publishing Company is part of the Maxwell Communication Group of Companies.

Printed in the United States of America

First Edition

10 9 8 7 6 5 4 3 2 1

CONTENTS

Chapter 1

A FIVE-YEAR STRUGGLE

The month of April 1945 was the beginning of the end of World War II in Europe. Great Britain and France had been at war with Germany since September 3, 1939. It was five years and seven months since the German attack on Poland started the largest war in history. The United States had joined the battle against Germany and Italy on December 8, 1941, the day following the Japanese attack on Pearl Harbor in Hawaii. U.S. armed forces had been at war for three years and four months. Russia had been in the war for three years and ten months following Germany's attack on the Soviet Union on June 22, 1941.

On D-Day, June 6, 1944, following major victories in North Africa and Italy, American and British armies landed on the beaches of Normandy in France. It was the start of the Allied conquest of Europe, taking it back from the Germans. At the same time, their ally to the East, Russia, was beginning to score one victory after another on Germany's eastern front.

The spring of 1945 brought more Allied victories that pushed Germany back within its borders. American, British, Canadian, French and Russian forces continued their successful advances from both the east and the west. Germany was finally on the verge of defeat.

But it had not always been that way.

A U.S. convoy rolls through Duren, just one of many German towns that had been reduced to rubble by Allied bombs and artillery fire.

Germany Overruns Western Europe

In September 1939 Germany invaded Poland. In five short weeks that nation became the first victim of German aggression. 1940 was a year of defeat and hard-fought defensive warfare for both Great Britain and its allies in Europe. In May of that year German dictator Adolf Hitler's German army, the Wehrmacht, attacked Belgium, Holland and France. The armies of these three nations as well as the British Expeditionary Force in France were all defeated quickly. Over 330,000 British and other Allied troops were evacuated to England from the French seaport of Dunkirk on June 1, 1940.

Hitler's panzers (tanks) continued their blitzkrieg "lightning war" attacks across France, forcing that country to surrender on June 25, 1940. In less than two months the Nazis had succeeded in occupying all of western Europe. They then began preparations to cross the English Channel and invade the British Isles.

The Battle of Britain

Great Britain now stood alone to fight the victorious Axis, as Germany and its ally Italy were called. Cut off from any help from the continent of Europe, Great Britain was dependent on supplies and reinforcements coming by sea. Canada, Australia and other British colonies rushed them supplies and reinforcements. The United States also began sending badly needed food and other supplies and equipment to its friend, Great Britain. As supply convoys crossed the Atlantic Ocean en route to the British Isles they were under constant attack by German U-boats (submarines) and aircraft of the Luftwaffe, the German air force.

Faced with the threat of an immediate invasion by German forces now stationed in France, Great Britain prepared for the worst. Its air force was its only defense. The Germans began regular bombing attacks on British cities and military bases. Under the command of Reichsmarshal

British rescue workers in London search for survivors in a bomb-damaged building following an air raid by the German Luftwaffe.

Hermann Goering, some 2,500 German aircraft set out to defeat the Royal Air Force (RAF) and prepare the way for Operation Sea Lion. This was the code name Hitler gave the planned invasion of Great Britain.

RAF Fighter Command Defeat the Luftwaffe

Following the first major raids by the Luftwaffe in July 1940, the RAF Fighter Command rose to the challenge. Suffering heavy losses in both pilots and aircraft, the RAF was still able to fight off the Luftwaffe attacks. By the fall of 1940 Hitler cancelled Operation Sea Lion because the Luftwaffe had failed to drive the RAF Spitfire and Hurricane fighter squadrons from the skies. Great Britain had won the Battle of Britain.

The RAF Bomber Command then went into action. Because the Luftwaffe had been bombing cities in England, the RAF started bombing German cities. Under the command of Air Marshal Arthur "Bomber" Harris, RAF bombers began nightly raids against German targets. The tide of battle was beginning to turn against the Nazis at last.

Germany Attacks in Russia and North Africa

Perhaps the biggest mistake Hitler made was to attack Russia. Although the German armies successfully invaded Russia on a 2,000-mile front, they were unable to fight on to a complete victory. The Russian armies and Russian people fought back valiantly. Eventually they took over the offensive and in 1943 the invading German armies began to be driven back.

During the same period the British were fighting a three-year-long series of battles against the Italian and the German armies in North Africa. Joined by U.S. forces in November 1942, they drove Axis forces from North Africa in May of 1943.

Allies Invade Italy and Normandy

The defeat of the Axis forces in North Africa was quickly followed by the invasion of the Italian island of Sicily and the Italian mainland. The Italians surrendered almost immediately but the German armies in Italy carried on the fight. The Allies continued their offensive, steadily driving the German armies northward during 1943, 1944 and 1945. The early victories in Italy were followed in June 1944 by D-Day in Normandy and the invasion of southern France.

The Allied armies had returned to mainland Europe with three successful invasions. At the same time the Russians were defeating the Germans all along the bitterly contested eastern front. After five years of war the end was drawing near. In March of 1945 General Dwight D. Eisenhower, the supreme commander of the Allied armies in western Europe, and Joseph Stalin, the Russian dictator, agreed on the final tactics that would result in the defeat of Germany.

By April 1945 the Allies had defeated the German armies on all fronts. The fate of Nazi Germany was sealed.

Chapter 2

EASTWARD FROM THE RHINE

The western Allies began their final advance into Germany in February 1945, following the defeat of Germany in the Battle of the Bulge in the Ardennes Forest of Belgium. Confronted by three major German army groups, their advances were slow. But eventually, the Rhine River, Hitler's main line of defense, was reached and British and U.S. forces in huge numbers were ready to cross it.

One major obstacle to the advance was the presence of huge dams on the River Roer. The British 21st Army Group and the U.S. 9th Army launched Operation Grenade to capture them. On February 9 the dams were all captured, but it was too late. Heroic Germans had sabotaged the flood gates and released torrents of water into the valley below. The flooded countryside extended for miles, blocking the Allied advance along a wide front. Finally, as the waters receded, Operation Grenade was able to complete its task on February 23 and advance beyond the Roer further into Germany.

The Rhine is Finally Crossed

The first crossing of the strategic barrier of the Rhine River occurred at Remagen, Germany, when the U.S. 1st Army seized a railroad bridge on March 7. A bridgehead was soon established and American troops crossed the Rhine in force. A few days later, the flamboyant American general George S. Patton, known to his men as "old blood and guts," led his U.S. 3rd Army across the Rhine in a surprise attack 100 miles to the south.

In the north, on March 23 Field Marshal Bernard Montgomery launched Operation Plunder. Canadian and British troops crossed the Rhine in force near the Dutch-German border. The next day British and American airborne divisions dropped paratroops to establish more Allied strongpoints east of the Rhine, further extending the British crossings. By the end of March 1945, U.S., British and French armies had all crossed the Rhine in strength and were driving ever deeper into Germany.

The Air War in Germany

During 1943 and 1944 the United States Army Air Force (USAAF) and the British RAF had established complete air superiority. Daylight attacks by USAAF B-17 and B-24 heavy bombers followed by nighttime raids by British Halifax, Wellington and Lancaster four-engine bombers destroyed German factories and cities. Supported by long-range American P-51 and P-47 fighters, they gradually destroyed much of Germany's remaining air force and many of its airfields.

By late 1944 the German Luftwaffe had lost most of its ability to fight the Allied aerial armadas. Short of fuel, ammunition, planes and pilots, it could no longer stop the huge

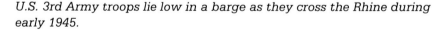

U.S. 3rd Army troops lie low in a barge as they cross the Rhine during early 1945.

A U.S. B-17 Flying Fortress over Germany after dropping bombs on a German airfield

Allied bomber fleets as they unloaded their deadly cargoes on German cities and military targets. Gradually, the air war shifted from high-level bombing raids to low-level bombing and strafing missions in support of the advancing Allied ground forces.

USAAF high-flying fighter escorts, P-51 Mustangs, P-47 Thunderbolts and P-38 Lightnings were all converted to fighter-bombers. Equipped with bomb and rocket racks in addition to their machine guns, they strafed and bombed the enemy constantly. RAF Typhoon, Mosquito and Beaufighter fighter-bombers were also brought into action.

German Luftwaffe Final Efforts

German first-line fighters, the Messerschmitt 109 and the Focke-Wulf 190, were being destroyed in ever-increasing numbers. Hitler finally called on two of his secret weapons. High-speed Me 262 and Ar 234 jet fighters, piloted by the few remaining skilled veterans, took to the air. Both of these fighters, the world's first operational jet aircraft, were faster than and superior to the Allied fighters in many ways. If they had been produced in quantity a year earlier, the air war over Europe might have turned out differently. However, too few and too late, these superior aircraft were finally grounded for lack of fuel.

Unlimited supplies and reinforcements for the Allies were flowing into Germany from the West. With the wings of the Luftwaffe thoroughly clipped, U.S. and British supply lines operated without interference from the air. Allied superiority over the Germans increased daily in every category. Meanwhile the enemy was short of food, fuel and ammunition. Hundreds of thousands of German fighting men had been lost in combat or were captured. They were being replaced by old men, teenaged boys and the sick and wounded who were still able to carry a gun.

With the once highly vaunted and feared Nazi forces defeated both in the air and on the ground, the final offensive in the West was about to begin. From the North Sea in Holland and Germany to the Alps mountain ranges in the south, the western Allies were ready to launch their final attacks into Germany.

Victorious American troops found unfinished He 162 jet fighters in an underground factory in a salt mine in Germany.

Chapter 3

THE RUSSIAN 1,000-MILE FRONT

By the summer of 1944 the Russian offensives on ten different fronts had achieved great success. Driving westward from central Russia, the victorious Russian armies had driven deep into Poland. By September 1944 they were knocking on the gates of Warsaw, the Polish capital. At the same time, German troops in Finland and their Finnish allies were being defeated. Far to the south on the Ukrainian front, German armies in Romania, Hungary and Bulgaria were also on the verge of defeat.

All along the thousand-mile front from the Gulf of Finland in the north to the Black Sea in the south the Nazi armies were in retreat. The Germans already were fighting a losing battle on the western front against the Americans, British and French. The wide-spread Nazi armies did not have the strength to fight off the now vastly superior Russian armies on the eastern front, too.

Victory in the Balkans

On September 1, 1944, the Allied air forces in southern Europe and the Mediterranean area began Operation Rat Week. They bombed and strafed the German forces in Greece, Yugoslavia and Bulgaria. It gave much-needed support to Yugoslavian and Greek partisans and to the Russian Ukrainian Front armies who were battling the Germans with great success.

Although the German armies in Romania launched fierce counterattacks in that area, they were quickly defeated.

Russian Marshal Rodion Malinovsky led his Ukrainian forces in an attack that forced the Germans to retreat hundreds of miles westward to the Hungarian border. At the same time civilian uprisings against the German occupation armies in Hungary and Czechoslovakia kept the Nazi armies there tied down fighting the resistance forces.

On September 9, Bulgaria, a long-time German ally, changed sides and joined the Russians. This enabled the Russians to attack through that country against German army groups in Greece and Yugoslavia, forcing them into further retreats.

By October 1 General Malinovsky's Ukrainian Front Army was driving deep into Romania. A communist government was set up in Bucharest, the capital of Romania. Some 40,000 German sympathizers were imprisoned or killed. On that date Hungarian officials traveled to Moscow to ask for peace. They wanted to save their people from the fate suffered by the Romanians. But the battles for Hungary continued for another month.

Although all the Balkan countries in southern Europe were in Russian hands by the end of 1944, the German Army Group South resisted with all its remaining strength. Budapest, the capital of Hungary, was still under siege at the end of December. It did not fall to the Russians until February 1945. The Russians were then ready to drive through Czechoslovakia and Austria toward Germany.

A German soldier throws a hand grenade as the Wehrmacht fights a losing battle against the advancing Russian hordes.

Russian tanks and infantry in huge numbers advanced steadily on all fronts.

On the Northern Front

On the Leningrad front the Russians began an offensive against the German Army Group North in mid-September 1944. In less than 30 days they had recaptured all three of the Baltic nations, Estonia, Latvia and Lithuania. They bypassed a large part of the German Army Group North which remained trapped on the Courland Peninsula in Latvia for the rest of the war.

Continuing the battles on the Baltic Sea, the Russians captured Riga, the capital of Latvia. The giant seaport of Memel in Lithuania was placed under siege as the Russians advanced around it into Germany's East Prussia. This was the first time Russian troops had set foot on German soil.

The Main Russian Offensive

The German Army Group A had held the center of the eastern front all through the fall of 1944. Their line stretched along the Vistula River that ran northward into the Baltic Sea through Poland. Finally, however, the Russian dictator Joseph Stalin ordered the Stavka (Moscow high command) to plan a major offensive to defeat that force.

The Russians, newly equipped with the latest weapons and thirsting for blood, were ready to attack. Their goal was to cross the Vistula and, using blitzkrieg tactics, advance all the way to Berlin, the capital of Germany, in just 45 days.

This giant offensive kicked off on January 12, 1945. Although warned by German Chief of Staff Heinz Guderian of Russian preparations along the Vistula, Nazi dictator Adolf Hitler paid no attention. He was concerned about problems in the Battle of the Bulge on the western front and major defeats in the Balkans. When the Russians did attack, the Germans were poorly prepared and were forced to retreat immediately.

Demoralized and defeated German troops in the Baltic countries and in East Prussia were temporarily trapped. Some 50,000 Nazi troops were evacuated by sea and landed at other German Baltic seaports well behind the fighting. Two huge German army groups, completely outgunned and short of supplies, were driven back along a 500-mile line. The Russians had crossed the Vistula River and by January 17, 1945, they had driven the German garrison from Warsaw, the capital of Poland.

Under the command of Marshal Georgi Zhukov, the great

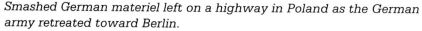

Smashed German materiel left on a highway in Poland as the German army retreated toward Berlin.

A Russian mortar company prepares to fire over advancing infantry.

Russian hero, and Marshal Konstantin Rokossovsky, the 1st and 2nd Belorussian Armies swept aside all German resistance. By January 29 they had crossed the German eastern border in force and reached the Oder River, only 50 miles from the German capital of Berlin. It had taken the Russians only 17 days to advance the 200 miles from the Vistula to the Oder. It had taken six months to advance the same distance in the last half of 1944. The German armies were in full retreat before the now vastly superior Russian army.

Russian Advances Halted Temporarily

Because the Russians had advanced such great distances in just a few weeks they were running short of supplies. They had to allow time for their supply line to form so that they could regroup, rearm and rest before making the final assault on Berlin. Furthermore, the advances toward Berlin had left Russian forces to the north and to the south far behind.

In the north some German forces guarding the Vistula line were still able to fight back in strength. Located in the

Russian infantry advance across open country to attack retreating German units.

northern Germany territory called Pomerania, they were commanded by the infamous SS Reichsfuhrer Heinrich Himmler. In addition to being head of the SS (*Schutz-staffen*—or protection squads) Himmler was second in command of all German forces. Only Hitler outranked him.

The Russian Stavka ordered the Russian armies in the north to concentrate on the defeat of Reichsfuhrer Himmler's armies. With General Rokossovsky in command, using large numbers of tanks and heavy artillery, the 2nd Belorussian Front Army advanced over 35 miles into Pomerania by February 24. The giant Russian T-34 tanks were more than a match for the German panzers. Joined by units from General Zhukov's armies attacking from the south, the Russians defeated the strong SS army and controlled most of East Prussia and Pomerania by March 16.

Meanwhile, in the south, the Nazi forces fared no better. Again the Stavka ordered the Russians to attack in strength. The Russian air force, now equipped with new aircraft and skilled pilots, led the way. Except for one small area in eastern Czechoslovakia, the Russians continued their rapid advance westward. Newly reinforced by Mongolian troops from eastern Russia, the Red Army forces annihilated the panzer armies of Army Group South. On April 13 the Russians entered Vienna, the capital of Austria.

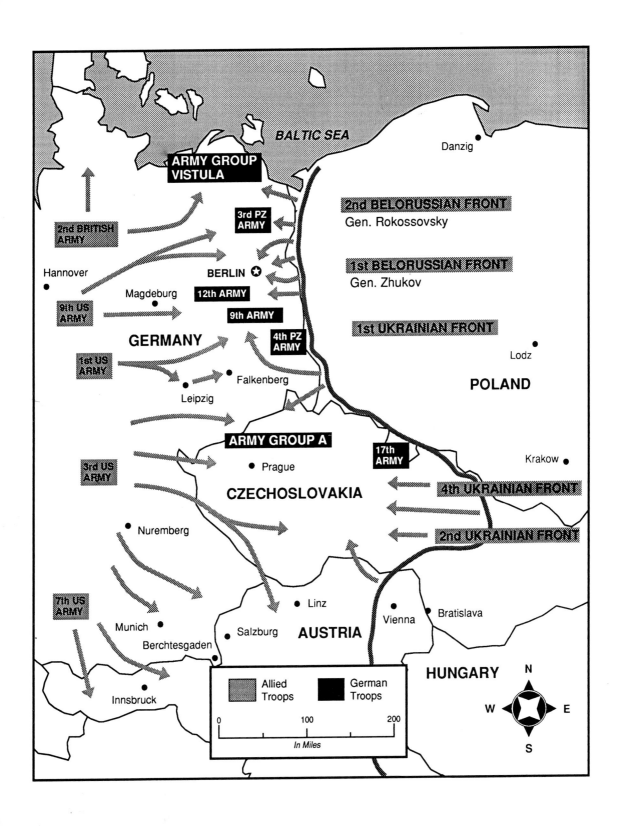

BALTIC SEA

Danzig

ARMY GROUP VISTULA

2nd BELORUSSIAN FRONT
Gen. Rokossovsky

2nd BRITISH ARMY

3rd PZ ARMY

1st BELORUSSIAN FRONT
Gen. Zhukov

Hannover

BERLIN ★

Magdeburg

12th ARMY

9th US ARMY

9th ARMY

1st UKRAINIAN FRONT

GERMANY

4th PZ ARMY

Lodz

1st US ARMY

POLAND

Leipzig

Falkenberg

ARMY GROUP A

17th ARMY

Krakow

3rd US ARMY

Prague

CZECHOSLOVAKIA

4th UKRAINIAN FRONT

Nuremberg

2nd UKRAINIAN FRONT

Linz

7th US ARMY

Vienna

Bratislava

Munich

Salzburg

AUSTRIA

Berchtesgaden

HUNGARY

Innsbruck

| Allied Troops | German Troops |

0   100   200

In Miles

N
W   E
S

Chapter 4

GERMANY SURROUNDED

The U.S. and British forces in western Europe had defeated the Germans as easily although not quite as dramatically as the Russians. In March 1945 General Eisenhower ordered General Omar Bradley's 12th Army Group to advance eastward across the Rhine River into central Germany. Their goal was to drive toward the German cities of Dresden and Leipzig and join up with Russian forces approaching from the east. If they succeeded, they would split the German armies in two.

The Russian leader, Joseph Stalin, was pleased with this action as it opened the way for Russian forces to advance toward the German capital of Berlin from the east. During the early months of 1945 the Russians had completed the conquest of Poland and were advancing into Germany. By March 1 they were well within the eastern border of Germany, driving the battered and defeated German armies before them.

British Advance in the North

Field Marshal Bernard Montgomery, commander of the British and Canadian forces, was unhappy with General Eisenhower's plans. With assistance from the U.S. 9th Army, he was planning for his 21st Army Group to advance through northern Germany and attack and capture Berlin. The forces under his command advanced across the Rhine River into Germany. The superbly trained and equipped Allied forces defeated the enemy at every turn.

American tanks rumble through another captured city as they drive deeper into Germany.

Meanwhile, a large German army blocked the path of the Allied forces in central Germany. Field Marshal Walther Model commanded the German Army Group B defending the industrial valley of the Ruhr. However, following combined attacks by the British from the north and U.S. forces from the west and south, this German force was completely overwhelmed.

The U.S. 9th Army under the command of General William Simpson and the U.S. 1st Army under the command of General Courtney Hodges scored a stunning victory. Some 325,000 German troops surrendered on April 18 and their commander, Field Marshal Model, committed suicide. The road to Berlin now appeared to be open for an attack by the British 21st Army Group and the rapidly advancing U.S. 1st and 9th Armies.

The River Elbe Halt Line

Sweeping all German resistance before them, the combined U.S. and British forces drove through Germany to the Elbe River. It was only 60 miles from Berlin at its closest point. By mid-April both British and American armies were ready to cross the river and continue on to Berlin. The U.S. 2nd Armored Division had already crossed the river at Magdeburg, Germany.

American soldiers (left) *and Russian soldiers congratulated each other on the defeat of Nazi Germany, as they met on a bridge over the Elbe River.*

British and American commanders in the field all sought permission to continue the advance. But the Allied supreme commander in the west, General Eisenhower, ordered them to halt and not to advance any farther eastward.

General Eisenhower was acting on two basic concerns. He feared that the western Allies and the Russians might clash with each other over who would capture Berlin. Secondly, he believed that the Nazis were building a "National Redoubt"—a heavily reinforced location in the Austrian Alps from which Hitler would lead his armies in a bitter last stand. This proved not to be the case.

As a result, all U.S. and British advances were stopped on the central and northern fronts of western Germany at the River Elbe. Meanwhile, south of Berlin, on April 25, 1945, U.S. and Russian troops met at the German town of Torgau and completed the joining of the two great Allied armies. The German armies had been cut in half. Central Germany and the German capital, Berlin, were now completely surrounded by the U.S., British and French armies advancing from the west and the Russian armies coming from the east.

Chapter 5

BATTLE
OF BERLIN

The coming Battle of Berlin was to be not only a military battle but a political battle as well. In early April the Russians had advanced to within 35 miles east of Berlin, ready to attack. At the same time, British and American forces were at the River Elbe "halt line" just 60 miles to the west of Berlin and were also ready and able to attack and capture Berlin.

During the period from February 4 to 11, 1945, President Franklin D. Roosevelt of the United States, Prime Minister Winston Churchill of Great Britain and the Russian dictator Joseph Stalin held a historic meeting at Yalta in the Crimea in Russia. There it was decided that the Soviet Union would control the eastern half of Germany after its surrender. Berlin was included in that area. The western Allies would control the western half of Germany.

The British wanted their 21st Army Group under the command of Field Marshal Montgomery to attack eastward and capture Berlin. They feared a revitalized Soviet Union and thought that the communists would eventually be an enemies. They knew that the Soviet Union would emerge from the ashes of World War II as a great world power and would try to control as much of Europe as possible.

On the other hand, the United States wanted Russia's cooperation in the war against Japan. So they were in favor of letting the Russians capture Berlin and were eager to make other concessions to the Soviet leaders. Little did they know that the Soviet Union would control most of eastern Europe, eastern Germany and part of Berlin until 1990.

American troops move cautiously through the ruins of a German village.

Eisenhower Makes the Final Decision

On March 28, 1945, General Dwight D. Eisenhower, as supreme commander of the western Allies, notified Joseph Stalin that the American and British attacks would be concentrated to the north and to the south of Berlin. Winston Churchill disagreed and was furious. He insisted that the British and Americans should meet the Russians as far east as possible. This meant taking Berlin before the Russians. Churchill was certain that the Russians could not be trusted.

However, General Eisenhower, basing his actions on agreements made at Yalta, still ordered the British to stay behind the Elbe River. The U.S. 1st and 3rd Armies under the command of General Hodges and General Patton launched an attack south of Berlin toward Leipzig and Dresden, defeating the Nazi forces as they advanced. This left the German capital at the mercy of the Russians.

The Bombing of Dresden

To further show their support of the Russians and to help in their offensive, the Allied commanders in western

American troops with a captured picture of Adolf Hitler and a Nazi flag.

Heilbronn, Germany, like Dresden, was one of the most devastated cities in all of Europe.

Europe ordered a bombing attack on Dresden, Germany. This was one of several German cities attacked to further weaken the Nazis' ability to carry on the war. On the night of February 13, 1945, the RAF sent more than 800 bombers to attack Dresden.

The RAF dropped some 2,700 tons of high-explosive and incendiary bombs and set the entire city ablaze with the worst firestorm of the war. USAAF bombers followed up with another attack the next day. The city was almost entirely demolished and it is estimated that some 50,000 people died, many of them refugees. A bombing raid of no direct military importance, it was one of the most shameful Allied attacks of the entire war. However, it did further weaken the German will to fight and it encouraged the Russians.

General Zhukov in Command

Stalin and the Stavka ordered the top Russian commanders back to Moscow to plan the final assault on Berlin. Marshal Zhukov was named to head the attack and was ordered to begin the final offensive in mid-April. Marshal Zhukov commanded the 1st Belorussian Front Army and was assisted by Marshal Ivan Konev, commanding the 1st Ukrainian Front Army. On April 16 they began their final attacks toward Berlin.

Preparing for this day, Nazi dictator Adolf Hitler had converted Berlin into a giant fortress. He was determined to defend the German capital to the death. He had personally assumed command of all German military activity and he spent all of his time in the German Command Post called the *Fuehrerbunker* which was located beneath his residence, the Chancellery.

Meanwhile, U.S., British and Russian bombers were attacking Berlin regularly. And when it finally became apparent that the British 21st Army Group would not be permitted to cross the Elbe, the Russians continued their advance to the outskirts of Berlin.

An American and a Russian soldier embrace in friendship. Unfortunately, these friends soon became enemies with the advent of the "cold war."

As the war drew to a close, German soldiers surrendered by the thousands every day.

Berlin Encircled

Marshal Zhukov's and Marshal Konev's armies advanced steadily. At the same time other Russian armies continued their attacks to the north and to the south to keep German armies from reinforcing the capital. To the west British and U.S. forces were also attacking with full force everywhere along the German line except toward Berlin.

On April 20, Hitler's birthday, the man who had wanted to control all of Europe gave final command responsibilities to his key generals. He stated, "Berlin stays German . . . , and Europe will never be Russian." That day was also his last public appearance outside of his command bunker. It soon became evident that the Russians had cut off Berlin from the north and south. On April 23 Hitler stated that he would rather commit suicide than surrender to the Russians. He planned to stay in Berlin until the end.

On April 25 the Russians completely surrounded Berlin. They had trapped and defeated two main German armies defending the city. German troops of all ages and description were fighting bitterly in the suburbs of the city, making a last-ditch effort to repel the attackers.

Hitler's Last Days

On April 26, the German 12th Army, located southwest of Berlin, made a valiant attempt to break through the Russian forces surrounding the city. Under the command of General Walther Wenck, they advanced from the southwest to within 15 miles of Berlin. However, it was too late. The Russian forces led by Marshal Zhukov were already within Berlin and approaching its heart.

In desperation, Adolf Hitler began firing his generals for their failure to defeat the Russians. Heinrich Himmler, his long-time friend and second in command, was removed from office. Other generals who continued to withdraw from the battle also were replaced. As the Russians approached the *Reichstag* (German government headquarters) and Adolf Hitler's residence, the Chancellery, Hitler remained trapped in his underground headquarters.

On April 29 as the final battles in central Berlin began, Adolf and his mistress, Eva Braun, were married. As one of his last official acts, the once-powerful Nazi leader appointed Admiral Karl Doenitz, commander in chief of the German navy, as the new head of the German government.

The next day Adolf Hitler and Eva Braun committed suicide. The *Reichstag* and the Chancellery fell to the Russians and the Battle of Berlin had ended.

Three days later, on May 2, 1945, Berlin surrendered. The Battle of Berlin had lasted only a few weeks but it was one of the bloodiest of the war in Europe. It produced some 300,000 Russian casualties and an unknown number of German military and civilian deaths. Over 500,000 German troops were captured during the battle.

Chapter 6

UNCONDITIONAL SURRENDER

Following the fall of Berlin it was only a matter of days until the entire German army would collapse. For a while the remaining German armies kept fighting, trying to save the German people from the advancing Russians. Almost everyone wanted to be captured by or surrender to the western Allies. It soon became a race between the British and American forces and the Russians to see which could accept the surrender of the various German armies.

German forces in Italy had already surrendered on April 29. U.S. and British forces had then joined up with Allied forces in France and Austria. They also joined forces with Marshal Tito's (Josip Broz) armies in Yugoslavia.

On May 2, 1945, British forces under Field Marshal Montgomery finally crossed the Elbe River and secured the Danish peninsula. Meanwhile, German troops remaining in Holland were completely cut off and ready to surrender. On May 4 Montgomery accepted the surrender of all German troops in Denmark, Holland and northwest Germany.

Other exciting events occurred during these final days

German officers preparing to surrender to British forces at an airport in the Netherlands.

Field Marshal Wilhelm Keitel (center) *and his staff prepare for the signing of the surrender papers for Germany.*

that marked the end of the war. Admiral Doenitz ordered all German U-boats and other ships of the German *Kriegs-marine* (navy) still at sea to return to their home ports and surrender. During the first week of May the RAF carried out Operation Manna, dropping food and medical supplies to starving Dutch civilians.

Surrender to the Western Allies Refused

Although many German units tried to surrender to British and American forces, many of them had to be rejected. General Eisenhower, bound by the agreements reached at Yalta between the three major Allied powers, could not accept surrender from German armies in Russian-held territory. These agreements called for a combined unconditional surrender of all German forces to a combined Allied surrender team made up of representatives of both the western Allies and Russia.

General Alfred Jodl was the official German representative in the final surrender negotiations. Meeting with General Eisenhower at Reims, France, on May 6, he suggested that the German armies be given an opportunity to avoid capture by the Russians and surrender to the United States or Great Britain. Trapped by political pressures, General Eisenhower had to refuse, but he did agree to allow another several days before all troops must surrender wherever they were located.

Admiral Doenitz agreed to an unconditional surrender under these terms. The official surrender document was signed at Reims on May 7, 1945, by representatives of the United States, Great Britain, France, Russia and Germany. However, the Russians insisted on having a second surrender ceremony the next day in Berlin. This ceremony was also attended by representatives of all Allied powers. As a result, Victory in Europe (VE) Day was celebrated on May 8 in Berlin a day after the official surrender had taken place. Hostilities officially ended in Germany on May 8, 1945, at 11:01 P.M.

Fighting Continues For Another Week

The German Army Group Centre in Czechoslovakia was surrounded on all sides by the Russians. They refused to comply with the Russian surrender demands. As a result, Russian Marshal Ivan Konev ordered attacks on the German army and on Prague, the capital of Czechoslovakia. Three days of fierce fighting went on until the Germans finally surrendered on May 11.

Other fighting continued in Austria and Yugoslavia as German Army Group E refused to surrender to the Russians. They, too, were trying to surrender to the Americans. Many were able to do so, although the Russians succeeded in capturing and obtaining the surrender of a number of German SS divisions. What remained of German Army Group E surrendered to Tito's Yugoslavian partisan forces on May 14.

Ruins of Hitler's seat of government— The Reichstag—following its
destruction during the fall of Berlin.

Admiral Doenitz, the new leader of Germany, was finally arrested by Allied forces on May 23 at the German naval base of Flensberg near Germany's border with Denmark. He had been allowed to remain free for an extra few days to supervise the surrender of German U-boats and other naval units.

With the surrender of Germany now behind them, the Allies could turn their attention to the Pacific war against Japan. They also had to work out what proved to be an uneasy peace in Europe, which was just the beginning of years of problems that were to come.

A jubilant American soldier hugs a motherly English woman in London, England, as they celebrate Germany's unconditional surrender.

Chapter 7

THE HOLOCAUST

Holocaust - *"A complete or thorough sacrifice or destruction, especially by fire"* Webster's Third International Dictionary

In 1933 the Nazis in Germany began persecuting members of the Jewish faith. Adolf Hitler started these activities by boycotting Jewish-owned businesses, banning Jews from holding public office and banning them from various professions. In addition Jews and their businesses were often attacked by young German Nazi gangs. At that time many German Jews began fleeing Germany to find new homes elsewhere around the world.

In addition to persecuting the Jews, Nazi Germany extended the same treatment to communists, gypsies, criminals, homosexuals, mental patients and others. Any person or group who was considered undesirable by the Nazi rulers was endangered. Anyone who was not a so-called "pure Aryan"—meaning white, Gentile and of northern European extraction—was suspect. Hitler believed that the German people who possessed these Aryan characteristics were a superior race and were destined to rule the world.

The most tragic and pathetic victims of World War II were the millions of innocent people who fell victim to the Nazi hatred of the Jews. It was truly a "holocaust," the name that has been given to the ongoing persecution and extermination of the millions of Jews and others by the Nazi regime before and throughout World War II. It was a tragic period in history for all mankind.

Slave laborers in the Buchenwald concentration camp, many of whom died of starvation before the U.S. troops freed the camp in April 1945.

Concentration Camps

The prison or work camps that housed the victims of Nazi persecution were called concentration camps. The first one, and that most remembered, was at Dachau in southern Germany. It was built in 1933. By 1937 two more were added at Sachsenhausen and Buchenwald. One exclusively for women was set up at Lichtenburg. Another one was built at Mauthausen, Austria, to house prisoners taken after the German takeover of that country in 1938.

These camps were meant originally to house German communist political prisoners, but they quickly were used for Jews also. Before the end of the war there were some 35 such camps throughout Germany and the countries they had occupied. In addition, there were six death camps used for killing Jews and other prisoners. However, those placed in the camps were often put to work in wartime industries. When too weak or sick to continue working, they were immediately put to death.

Crystal Night

Adolf Hitler began preaching hatred of the Jews as early as 1925 in his book *Mein Kampf*. Hitler, along with many others, blamed the Jews for the loss of World War I and the bad times that followed. He continued to preach anti-Semitism (hostility towards all things Jewish) as the Nazi party achieved greater and greater power in Germany. In 1933, after gaining full power as a dictator, Hitler issued orders restricting the activities of most Jews in Germany. Jewish doctors and lawyers were forbidden to practice their professions. Professionals in many other trades were expelled from their jobs. Eleven cities had walled sections called ghettos in which all Jews residing there were forced to live.

The Nuremberg Laws were passed in 1935, depriving Jews of full German citizenship. Thereafter, Jews were merely "subjects." Marriage and sexual relations between Jews and Aryans were forbidden. All Jews had to wear identification in the form of the yellow Star of David sewn on their clothing. Other "undesirables" wore similar markings to distinguish them.

Persecution continued at all levels of society. It reached a climax on the night of November 9, 1938, which came to be called *Kristallnacht* (crystal night) from the thousands of storefront windows that were broken. German storm troopers and plain thugs destroyed and plundered Jewish shops by the hundreds.

Using the excuse that a German diplomat had been killed by a Jew, the rioting began. It was a night of rampage when windows were smashed, Jews assaulted, stores and homes looted and Jewish synagogues burned.

Many Jews who had the money bought their way to freedom outside of Germany. Others who could not afford such action or who truly believed things would improve stayed and died. Fearful of criticism from peace-loving countries around the world, Hitler held off greater persecution of the Jews until the war started.

The remains of German Jews and other captives were found in huge furnaces that were used to incinerate the helpless victims.

Death Squads and Death Camps

As German blitzkrieg attacks drove deep into Poland and later into Russia, the Jewish problem increased. Both of these countries had large Jewish populations who suffered anti-Semitism from their own countrymen.

To deal with the additional number of Jews, Heinrich Himmler, head of the German SS, formed SS action squads called *Einsatzgruppen*. Local groups in the newly conquered lands were incited to riot against their Jewish neighbors. As each village and city was captured by the Germans, the Jews were rounded up. Many were shot by the squads and others were killed by gas in special trucks.

Some one million Jews were killed in this manner in 1941. As the job became too great for the SS troops to handle, special death camps were built for the specific purpose of using gas as a weapon of extermination. The infamous town of Auschwitz, in Poland, was the first camp created for that purpose.

Top German Leaders Responsible

With the complete encouragement of Adolf Hitler, the systematic extermination of Jews in Germany and its occupied territories was carried out by high-ranking German leaders. Heinrich Himmler was in overall charge of the units that carried out the horrendous task of eliminating the Jews. He was responsible for the death camps throughout the war. Captured at the end of the war as he tried to escape, he committed suicide.

Adolf Eichmann was given the job of putting the extermination of the Jews into effect. He was put in charge of the Office of Jewish Resettlement. He arranged for the transport of Jews and other prisoners to various work and/ or death camps. He was responsible for organizing the camps and the ultimate death of millions of people imprisoned in them. He escaped from Germany at the war's end and traveled to South America. He was discovered there by Israeli agents who kidnapped him in 1960. Tried in Israel, he was convicted of his war crimes and executed.

Other less fortunate victims were sent to camps where they were met by medical teams. Treated almost kindly at first, they were ultimately used for medical experimentation of incredible cruelty that resulted in their deaths. Dr. Josef Mengele, known as "the Angel of Death," was condemned by fortunate death-camp survivors who told of his gruesome work.

The Final Tally

The total number of lives lost in Germany's efforts to eliminate the Jews will never be known. The activities of the Germans were so varied and widespread that no accurate accounting can be made. As the war drew to a close German commanders ordered many camps in the east destroyed and their remaining prisoners marched westward toward concentration camps in Germany. Many of the prisoners were killed or died during the march.

As camps were liberated, the Allies realized that a true Holocaust had taken place. They had known of the existence of the camps but had not realized the complete horror of the situation. They were shocked by what they found. The true facts were beyond their wildest imagination.

The American troops who first entered the camps were struck dumb with horror. Barracks were filled with starving men, women and children waiting for their turn in the gas chambers. Outside, those already dead were stacked in piles like cordwood. Based on eyewitness accounts, interviews with survivors and by scrutiny of camp records that had not been destroyed, the Allies were able to determine what actually had taken place.

The years of the Holocaust had been a living hell. Some estimate that some 5 to 6 million Jews perished in German death camps. An equal number probably died in Poland and Russia. In addition, hundreds of thousands of Gentiles who also fell into the trap of German extermination policies were killed. The Holocaust, as it is now called, was the greatest crime in history.

Guarded by Allied military police, German leaders accused of war crimes sit in the defendant's dock during the Nuremberg trials.

Chapter 8

THE COST OF THE WAR

Although the war was to go on for several more months in the Pacific, the costs of the European conflict were already astronomical. Germany and Italy were the defeated enemy and much of both countries lay in ruins. However, the war had covered all of Europe, the British Isles and North Africa, leaving terrible destruction and suffering in all nations involved.

The death toll alone does not tell the whole story although it is the most readily understood statistic. Russia suffered the greatest losses of any nation with some 20 million killed. Poland came next with 6 million dead while Germany, the main aggressor, lost 5 million. In the Balkan states, Yugoslavia lost some 1,400,000 dead and its neighbors, Hungary, Bulgaria, Romania and Greece, lost almost as high a number.

The western European nations of France, Holland, Belgium and Luxembourg lost close to 1 million while Great Britain suffered a loss of some 400,000. The Scandinavian countries of Denmark, Norway and Finland had only about 100,000 killed while the central European nations of Czechoslovakia and Austria lost nearly 700,000.

The United States, as the latest and strongest arrival in the European war, had about 200,000 troops killed.

Civilian Losses Impossible to Measure

In addition to the incalculable number of Jews destroyed in the Holocaust and elsewhere, millions of other European civilians also died. With the complete destruction of cities, towns and villages, no accurate death count could be made. Millions of civilians were displaced as they became refugees. Without food and shelter, many died of disease and hunger.

Major cities, industries and businesses were destroyed indiscriminately in all countries where fighting occurred. The losses cannot be measured in dollars and cents. Some countries never recovered completely from their ecomomic losses suffered during the war. Great Britain, although never invaded, had suffered severe bombings. They were almost ruined financially at the end of the war.

The Cold War

The greatest cost of World War II was the complete breakdown of relations between western and eastern Europe. Although allies as long as the war was being fought, the relationship between communist Russia and its former comrades—the United States, Great Britain and the countries of western Europe—changed as soon as the war in

The war-shattered cities of Europe began to rebuild immediately. However, the threat of war would remain for almost 50 years as the "Cold War" between communist and noncommunist countries went on.

Europe ended. The Soviet Union was a giant communist nation whose goal was to rule the world. With the war over, the western democracies became its enemies.

As the war in Europe ended, control of Germany was divided among the four Allied nations—Russia, the United States, Great Britain and France.

Russia also controlled the eastern nations, made up of all of the Soviet Union's 16 member states, Poland, East Germany, Czechoslovakia, Romania, Hungary, Bulgaria and Yugoslavia. On the other side of the imaginary wall dividing all of eastern and western Europe were the nations of the western bloc, consisting of Great Britain, France, West Germany, Belgium, Holland, Norway, Finland, Denmark and Italy. Eventually a real wall was built between East and West Germany, reflecting the division in Europe itself between east and west.

Switzerland, Sweden, Spain and Portugal, all of which had remained neutral during the war, tended to side with the West in their relations after 1945.

The war was over but a new war was beginning— the "Cold War"—in which nations all over the world would side with either the communist nations led by the Soviet Union or the democratic nations led by the United States and Great Britain.

Although the Cold War never developed into a fighting war, both sides remained armed to the teeth. Each developed atomic bombs and all nations lived in constant fear of a nuclear holocaust that would follow a third world war.

World War II ended in Europe in May 1945. However, its aftershocks have been felt for almost 50 years. Only as this book is being written is the peace that should have happened in 1945 finally settling over the embattled continent of Europe. It can only be hoped that the six long years of war, the Holocaust and the cost to all nations in lives and devastation will not be forgotten —and will never, ever be repeated.

A Closer Look at . . .
THE ALLIED LEADERS

(above) *Prime Minister Winston Churchill of Great Britain, President Franklin D. Roosevelt of the United States and Premier Joseph Stalin of the Soviet Union* (seated left to right) *during the Big Three Conference at Yalta in the Russian Crimea in February 1945.*

(below) *Marshal Zhukov* (center), *the Russian commander during the attack on Berlin, celebrates victory with General Eisenhower and Field Marshal Montgomery* (on Zhukov's right).

GLOSSARY

Allies The nations that joined together during World War II to defeat Germany: Great Britain, the United States, the Soviet Union and France.

Aryan The "super-race" that Hitler and many Germans believed they belonged to.

blitzkrieg Means "lightning war" in German.

Cold War The state of political and military tension existing between Soviet Union dominated countries and the United States and its World War II allies.

concentration camps Work camps or prisons used by the Germans during World War II to house Jews and other so-called undesirables.

Fuehrer "Leader" in German. Hitler was called *der Fuehrer*.

Holocaust The term used to describe the extermination of Jews and others by the Germans during World War II.

jet fighter An airplane powered by a jet engine.

Kriegsmarine The German navy.

Luftwaffe The German air force before and during World War II.

Nazi A person or idea belonging to the German National Socialist party.

panzer A German tank.

reich The German government, or empire.

Reischstag The building housing the main offices of the German government in Berlin.

stavka The military high command of the Russian army during World War II.

U-boat German submarine.

Wehrmacht The German army.

INDEX